LET'S GET
REAL

LET'S GET
REAL

Are You Consciously Living Your Life Or
Is Your Life Subconsciously Directing You?

LINDA RAINWATER

XULON PRESS

Xulon Press
2301 Lucien Way #415
Maitland, FL 32751
407.339.4217
www.xulonpress.com

Unless otherwise indicated, Scripture quotations taken from the Holy Bible, New International Version (NIV). Copyright © 1973, 1978, 1984, 2011 by Biblica, Inc.™. Used by permission. All rights reserved.

Printed in the United States of America.

ISBN-13: 978-1-6628-0507-3

Table of Contents

Introduction

WHEN MY CHILDREN WERE GROWN, I RETURNED TO OUR EDUCATION system to acquire that sought-after piece of paper that influences how others evaluate you, how they shape their perception of your worth.

I obtained a degree in Accounting and one in Business Management, graduated Phi Theta Kappa and on the Dean's List. At the time this seemed to mean a lot. Then I found myself interested in other areas of study. I began taking classes for certification in Occupational Instruction and Psychology. Then circumstances redirected my focus and I became an Administrator for a non-profit.

Many of the areas of human behavior stuck in my mind. I even acquired the certification for a first level registered counselor. Human behavior can be very interesting and exasperating. What drives or directs people's lives? Why do different people react or respond so differently to similar circumstances or situations?

I never forgot one report I was working on, while still in school, about "progression" (in human behavior). I found an article that basically stated (as an example of progression) that a large

% of people that smoked also drank (alcohol); and a large % of people who drank also frequented bars and nightclubs; and a large % of people who attended bars and nightclubs did so with immoral or illegal activities in mind; and a large % of these people progressed into addiction, adultery or illegal substance activity. All of this demonstrated *progressive negative behavior*, a continual influence of declining moral or "love" perception of life and fellow man.

This concept of influence has always bothered me. Many many years later maybe this is what lead up to this book. It seems influence is a driving force that shapes our lives without us realizing it. Maybe we would make a few choices differently if we recognized the mental process of our daily lives. It all boils down to choice.

CHAPTER 1

Leading or Being Lead

NEVER BEFORE HAS MAN DEVELOPED THE TECHNOLOGY advancements we are experiencing today. Science and the Medical industries are at an all-time high in advancements. The innovations and ability of man is hard to keep up with.

The education and resourcefulness of man continues to escalade. Productivity seems to have no limits. The society of man is a strong resourceful force—something to be reckoned with. This has pushed man's expectations, dreams, desires and lusts to new heights.

Individually, this new man is self-determined and self-reliant. He is independent—free from the influence of others. Or is he? Have you ever heard the term, "... forever growing wiser yet weaker..."? What could this possibly mean or have to do with anything?

Even 'thou man has accomplished so much, and has reached strides of excellence, he has given in to weakness when it comes to his own mind. Weak because he now relies on electronic devises to do simple or mundane tasks; adding and subtracting, mathematical equations and formulas, spelling and definitions, simple memory tasks like phone numbers and address' or codes and password, and so on. Ever heard of "OK Google" or "Alexia"!

Following "hype" and popular opinion has become the way to go. Default is the new Go To. Gang and Peer pressure over ride common sense. Theory and Philosophy replace facts and reality. Public consensus has become the deciding factor.

Instead of checking out an opinion ourselves, we defer to tradition, culture, community or social standards, whatever influence is stronger. We don't even recognize or acknowledge that we are being influenced in any way. That might contradict our resolve of self-reliance and independence. Remember, "The squeaky wheel gets the grease" or the attention.

What we see on the internet or on TV far outweighs firsthand experience and knowledge. Sensationalized news and media stories sway our opinions and outlooks. World events and circumstances affect our fears and compassions. Our emotions override facts and reality. Feelings are more meaningful than written or established facts. Suggestions become our unthought out actions. Ever heard of "mob-mentality"!

Being our own man; standing for what we as an individual believes; relying on our own efforts to seek out truth; using the natural senses and purposes we were created with; these things are becoming obsolete. It is no longer right to be an independent thinker; it is conform, conform, conform.

Excessive outward boldness has become a common cover-up for insecurity and low self-esteem, which is manifested in aggressive actions to achieve power and control. What you see is not always what you get. What is said is not always what is done. A person's name and word are not always honorable.

We live in a time of deceit and counterfeit. Reality is covered with falsehood. Trust is conditional. Man isn't what he could be or what he portrays himself to be.

The diversity of the influences that cloud and complicate our choice is a confirmation that someone/something desires to win our choice (our vote) and that our choice must have great value or ramifications. Why is our choice so important?

When you start to study human behavior scholars will tell you that there are various types of behavior developed through experiences and exposures (and so on). Concluding that our lives/choices are divided into syndromes (signs and symptoms that are correlated with each other and often with a particular disorder), from the Greek word meaning "concurrence", closely linked (as in inherited syndrome).

When humans are studying or judging (classifying) other humans, they like to label things so they feel more confident in their conclusions or diagnosis (people who act like this have this syndrome; people who act like that have that syndrome). All bad or unexcepted behavior is usually classified as *deviant behavior*—characteristics of an evil person/lifestyle. High moral or heroic behavior is usually classified as *good behavior*—characteristics of an angelic person/lifestyle. Here again we come down to two basic categories.

Behavior is the consequence of the choices we make. Our choices are the manifestation of the greatest influences in our life. Our mind has the deciding factor to the influences that bombard us. The human mind is a powerful thing. Influence over it is coveted. So, we must be diligent about what we allow into our minds. We can forfeit the power of our minds (and our lives). We can allow our minds to be clouded, distorted, confused or dysfunctional without even recognizing it.

Our thoughts drive us. Our emotions direct us. But our thoughts and emotions are not always factual or permanent, clear or precise. So, we can mislead ourselves. Desires and feelings can change in an instant and pull us in a different direction all together. We cannot go aimlessly through life, being tossed "to and fro", we must take some accountability for ourselves and consciously participate in every aspect of our lives.

Do we even know what is real? Do we really know what is truth? Do we know how to be self-sufficient or independent? Are we living our own lives or are our lives leading/driving us?

CHAPTER 2

What is Influence

INFLUENCES ARE PART OF OUR EVERYDAY LIVES. AN INFLUENCE is the power to affect others; the power to produce affects without using force; the power to affect behavior.

Influences are around us each and every day, all day and night (24 / 7). Some influences we recognize, but most influences go undetected. Everything and everyone around us wants to sway us to their agenda or purpose. (Influence is a force around us, a force to persuade.)

These influences can be positive (good things) or negative (bad things). Because 'influence' does something (persuades or affects your thoughts or actions) it can't be an inanimate object.

It does something so it must be a live thing. As an example: a rock sitting on the ground, on its own cannot influence you to do something; but if someone is 'influenced' to pick up that rock and throw it at you, that action can influence your feelings or response.

Another example is the old cartoon with a little devil sitting on the left shoulder of the cartoon character and a little angel sitting on the right shoulder of the cartoon character, each trying to persuade the cartoon character to do what they want them to (their agenda or purpose). If the influences around us are trying to get us to do opposite or different things, there must be two agendas or purposes.

Some of the influence we feel is to do things that aren't nice or right. Maybe it is something that will hurt or discourage someone else. Maybe it is not legal or moral. Or, maybe it is something that will benefit others. Maybe it is something that will make someone very happy. Maybe it is something that will make us feel better. These agendas can basically be divided into two general categories—good and evil or bad.

As well as two categories, you could say there are three main sources of influence:

1. Our self; the desires, opinions and lusts of our own flesh or our own mind
2. Other people, the dictates or ways of the world, life circumstances
3. Unseen or undetected or spiritual force

An unseen influence or force is defined as a spirit. As an example, the spirit of unity.

Influence can be in your face – "if you don't give me that ball, I am going to hit you."

Or it can be subtle – "I've always heard how nice you are, so I know you are going to share your candy with me." The flattery or soft approach will make you feel as thou you aren't losing anything. But if it is a demand you may become defensive or fearful. Influences are not always obvious; we can miss it because we get caught up in what we are doing and don't pay attention to why we are doing it.

There is a well-known Conference speaker named, Dr. Bob Harrison (nick named Dr. Increase) who has spoken at our Church several times. On one visit he shared a story about himself that caught my attention. He said he was out of town to speak at a large conference and as he was settling in at his hotel room, he noticed he had forgot his tooth paste. So, he called down to the front desk to inquire about some toothpaste. They sent some up to his room right away. But it wasn't his brand. So, he got his shoes and jacket and walked to the nearest drug store and bought some toothpaste. As he was walking back to the hotel, he asked himself why he had to get this brand of toothpaste. He remembered that the brand he bought was the only brand his mother would buy as he was growing up and he had continued buying as an adult.

This prompted him to do some research on the reasons behind our choices (human behavior).

He was shocked to learn that 94% of our choices or decisions are due to outside influences. We may think we are making up our own mind, but influences have already shaped our perspective. The words, opinions, habits or motives of others around us have silently conformed us to their ways and their thinking.

We get so caught up in 'doing things as usual' or 'thinking the same way as usual', that we become unaware of why we are doing it. We don't see the influence. We don't connect the dots. Our pride would never let us believe or admit we have conformed to someone else's opinions or ways.

If someone tells you every day that tomatoes don't taste good, pretty soon you will avoid eating tomatoes because you expect them to taste bad. You won't notice that you changed your opinion to match someone else.

Another example: Joey doesn't get along with Billy or Ronny; so, he tells you that Billy and Ronny are mean to him; you become angry with Billy and Ronny even though they have never done anything to you and you have never seen them do anything to Joey. You just conformed to the influence or opinion of Joey.

Furthermore, when influence teams up with manipulation it is easier to see the potential of influence on our lives. Influences are not always deliberate, but manipulation is a deliberate attempt to get you to believe or to do (act on) someone else's agenda or motive.

Manipulation is a subtle influence. Manipulation can become a skill. Some can get so good at manipulation that it becomes their "go to" or life style. Just as lying can become a habit (as in habitual liar) manipulation can become habitual.

Manipulation is the means to an end, the bidding or desire of the one manipulating. The ones who manipulate the most are the ones who will never admit to or acknowledge this type of behavior (it is a secret skill to get what you want, so you can't admit it). It is a self-serving, self-justifying, self-gratifying action. This is one-way influence can be a bad or evil thing.

Manipulation is a behavior; behavior is learned by observation and teaching. If you observed a family member (as you were growing up) using the art of manipulation (through influence) to get what they wanted, you will probably think this is normal or acceptable behavior. And it benefits you, so you will probably become a manipulator yourself. Sometimes without the conscious thought or plan to do anything wrong or evil, or self-serving.

Emotional blackmail is a form of manipulation (influencing others to do what you want them to do). Simply put, emotional blackmail is threatening something negative or bad if the person does not do or believe the way you want them to. Emotional blackmail is most common in some sort of relationship. Example: in a relationship – one person threatens to leave the other person if they don't quit nagging.

It becomes easier to see that outside influences do affect our decisions. And some influences are more obvious than others. Some are deliberate and still others can be undeliberate. Either way these forces that shape our decisions and choices are outside of our own independent thinking. It can be humbling or very concerning that we are so vulnerable when it comes to conceding or submitting control over our lives or part of our lives to another.

We raise our children to go to 'school' and be taught what an organized group of people have decided we need to know about different subjects; history of our forefathers, certain or popular scientific beliefs, culture and governing practices of the country we live in, what is socially or sexually correct, and so much more. Skip ahead in any generation and what we are taught has and will change to what this organized group wants us to believe, this is influence in action. And now it becomes clearer to us that 'influence' is something we need to be aware of, it does affect every area of our lives.

Weather we address the reader as you, to make it more personal, or as we, to remind us that everyone is affected by influences, consciously identifying and managing the influences is the important thing we need to do.

CHAPTER 3

Common Bond

CULTURE IS ACTUALLY A TRAINING OF THE MIND. IT IS AN ATMOsphere that is created through influence.

Culture is generally meant to be a common interest or a united feeling (or the 'spirit' of a place or around a thing), sometimes a produced feeling in a place. The culture of a place is like the personality of a person; "it's just who we are or what we do". (While in Rome, do as the Romans).

Culture is something that is taught or developed. Culture becomes automatic because it is the general response, acceptance or concept. Culture defined: shared beliefs and values of a group; the beliefs, customs, practices and social behavior of a group; a particular set of attitudes that characterizes a group of people.

What is programed in us becomes our natural behavior or reactions produced by our experiences or the examples around us, as well as deliberate teaching and instructions.

This can be radicalization, which is a far more dangerous and deviant form of manipulation and emotional blackmail. It is a subtle insertion or replacement of personal values, perceptions and beliefs. This would include mob-mentality, which happens when the emotional beliefs and manifested actions of a group becomes an overpowering force that sweeps others up and into the agenda, it is being submitted to the aggressive perspective of a motivated group.

Mob-mentality is a "spirit" of entitlement or justification that makes it alright to have negative or hateful opinions or actions, outside influence swaying you to the "dark side". Without others siding and agreeing with you, you might not ever act on such feelings or opinions, but you have leaned to the consensus of the majority.

Successful marketers have learned how to create a "culture" around a product in order to promote that product and develop faithful customers. Starbucks, for instance, has been very successful at creating what is now called a "Coffee Culture" in the Seattle area as well as around the world. When people hear "Starbucks", their minds automatically start painting a picture of a warm, comfortable gathering place to meet friends or co-workers for work or pleasure while enjoying a warm (or cool) tasteful beverage, and maybe a sweet snack, as they relax and converse. The service is purposely aimed at making you feel important and taken care of. No wonder people want to come back.

In the 1950's the comfort beverage was hot chocolate (with marshmallows); before that "Tea Time". The beverage of choice may be different but the expected experience was and is very similar. People enjoy positive experiences, especially when enjoyed with others. Culture draws people together.

Our culture drives us to seek "like" thinking and behavior. Our human nature desires those people and things that agree with our way of thinking or our way of doing things. This common bond can keep us united, affirming one another's beliefs weather those beliefs are right or wrong. We bring these common beliefs into every area of our lives, and through us we are influencing others to agree with the culture we come from.

Just as influences can be to do good or to do evil; culture can lead us into positive behavior or negative behavior. We can be influenced by our own desires and lusts (our own flesh or ego), and we can be influenced through the culture of other people, society or the world. In order for us to steward our own lives and make the right choices for the success of our future we need to live conscious lives, determining our choices and decisions on merit and worth not just on the influence or culture of others, the hype. We can't live our lives on a conveyer belt being driven to a destiny we never desired or chose. Don't get led into an unproductive or harmful lifestyle. The choice is ours; we are not shackled to influences or culture.

Culture is unlimited because it is based only on a common interest or desire. Just look at a couple of things that can be considered culture:

Music	Food	Fashion	Movies	TV Shows	Hair Styles
Brands or Store Names	Way you handle money	Values & Morals			
Political Opinions	Generational Welfare Lifestyle	Criminal Lifestyle			
Sociopath Lifestyle	Gang Affiliation	Drug Usage	Attitude Toward Marriage		
Faith & Beliefs	Education	Careers	Sports	Facebook	

America was founded with a culture of social and religious freedoms. But America was also founded on the culture of Capitalism—free enterprise/enterprise culture. An economic and political system in which a country's trade and industry are controlled by private owners for profit. Private ownership of capital goods, by investments that are determined by private decisions, and by prices, production and distribution of goods that are determined mainly by competition in the free market. Simply put: individuals or partners are free to start their own business and work it to obtain the highest profit level possible determined by their investment (financial, time, labor and promotion).

Over the years the culture of capitalism/free enterprise overpowered the culture of social and religious freedoms. The two governing parties formed to protect the freedoms of the white-collar citizens (business men) and the blue-collar citizens (laborers) got caught up in the success of the capitalistic culture. The financial success determined influence and authority which determined power. The parties started focusing on the power and no longer on the citizens until the focus became battling one another for supreme power. This focus and battle for power will destroy the culture of Capitalism and freedom of the citizens. Free enterprise and your freedom to live where and how you please will be replaced by those who gain supreme power and how they choose to 'influence' or dictate your life. Remember, manipulators only want what benefits them (not anyone else). See how broad scoped influence can become the new culture.

Think about this; in our political system activists are paid to influence politicians to implement policies and laws that benefit the group or organization paying them. This puts a "value" on influence. Remember, you can not give special or specific rights to one group without infringing on the rights of everyone else. This is just another way to understand the impact of influence on our lives.

Power and authority can be good and bad at the same time. It can build self-confidence and be used to do a lot of good. Or it can build entitlement and justifies all self-will, evil decisions and works.

The battle for power and control is often approached in the same way as radicalization. Some may use the term "mob-mentality". The subtle influence to bind people together for a common cause. A "Party" or entity will use propaganda to make targeted groups believe they have their interests (and commonality) in mind. They especially target minority groups as they are more vulnerable to the need of affirmation and community. Yet the "Party" or entity is actually vying for the physical or financial support for their agenda (or votes to provide more influence or position). It is the game of influence through manipulation to serve the purpose of the manipulator. Sound like a merry-go-round?

To get off the merry-go-round we must take our thoughts and choices back and actually "think" before we react or form an opinion. We must be accountable for our thoughts, attitudes, beliefs and choices in order to protect ourselves from sensationalized influences.

Do we want to live our lives according to hype or facts? Who is really making our choices?

And it goes on and on. So, we must take control of what we allow to influence us if we are going to make positive choices for ourselves and our families. There are consequences for not paying attention to what and why we are doing certain things. We must take some accountability for our own lives. We are not victims, we have a choice, think and respond or don't think and just react.

There are even more influences that are similar to culture we need to be aware of. They work in the same way but the source is considered different, so don't overlook them. Tradition is an influence and a training of the mind. Tradition is a behavior or reaction that is handed down, generation to generation; group to group; community to community and so forth. They are the customs and/or beliefs of a group continued over a long period of time (long established tradition). We don't even question it; it is just tradition.

Traditions dictate behavior through familiarity and general acceptance or requirement. No thought or education is necessary to follow traditions. We don't even identify why we do or believe something, that's just the way we have always done it.

Long established traditions are hard to change (in people) as they have an emotion of "being loyal" attached to them. Simply put (the synonym for tradition)—habit. It is well established that most people do not like change. There are books on the topic of the resistance to change, the struggle with change, the difficulty in changing our mindsets. Human nature does not handle change easily, it creates stress. Breaking a long-standing habit requires great effort and conscious choices.

Education is an influence. We accept education as a good thing and an advancement not just an influence. But education is based on facts known or assumed at a particular time, by a particular group of people (those in control of our educational system). But how many times have things we have heard or been taught turn out later to be partially or completely wrong or in error (days, years or decades later). The same can be said of anything we hear or see on TV, on the Internet, in News

Papers and so on. Current affairs always have emotion and opinion mixed in. Today things taught in education and even past and current affairs are being changed to support or fit specific agendas not standards.

All these influences in our lives; opinions and beliefs, manipulation and emotional blackmail, culture and tradition, family values and morals, philosophies and theories, public / social media and news, our own attitudes and suppressed memories can all be managed so we aren't run over by them. The number of influences around us is hard to determine. Just understand that we are not the stand-alone, independent individuals we thought we were. We must think, choose, and take charge of our own lives.

Tell a lie long enough and people will believe it. Change the desired teaching of history and culture and you can change multiple generations. Influence has been here since the beginning of time and it's not going anywhere, it is sticking around and getting craftier and stronger all the time.

CHAPTER 4

There's a Science to it

SOME SCIENTISTS ARE NOW TEACHING US THAT MANKIND IS MADE up of mind, body and soul. Calling our mind our thought center or beginning of our thinking; our soul is our emotions and feelings or our spiritual being; our body is our human body or flesh and organs (including the brain).

Dr. Caroline Leaf has spoken at our Church several times. She is a Cognitive Neuroscientist with a PhD in Communication Pathology. She has authored multiple books, including, *Who Switched Off My Brain.*

She explains that science has concluded that our thought process starts in the mind. We are created with the ability to identify thought as one of two categories; fear or love. When a thought first comes to our mind, we have the ability to accept or reject the thought (free choice). If we reject the thought, it goes away. If we accept the thought, it is transferred to the brain (physical organ within the flesh-based body). The brain then reacts to the category of the thought (fear or love), causing a release of chemicals and hormones from the brain into the body, and these cause physical reactions in the body.

Then the brain stores these thoughts in the subconscious. These memories look like tree branches in scientific studies. Fear thoughts appear as trees with no leaves, withered and dark. Love thoughts appear as trees with flourishing leaves, alive and well. These subconscious thoughts come back to the conscious state when stirred up (by trigger points) to affect us all over again. This creates patterns and influences our thoughts and choices.

Our thought life has a direct effect on our physical wellbeing. It has been estimated that 84% of all illness in our bodies are directly connected to our thought life. Amazing as it seems, as we think so are we. Our thoughts and feelings cause physical reaction and releases in our bodies.

Because we have a free will choice to accept or reject thoughts, and because thoughts are either fear based or love based, we have the ability to manage our entire thought process. If our thought process affects our physical life, we have a high stake in taking care of our thoughts and choices. We can't afford to overlook influences, why we make the choices we do, what we have allowed our attitude to become. Remembering that 94% or our choices and decisions are due to outside influences is enough to make us stop and think.

Dr. Leaf made this statement, *"You have to develop a disciplined thought life, and part of that is increasing your awareness of what you are allowing into your mind."*

Can you believe that disciplining our thought lives can affect our attitudes? Our attitudes are a manifestation of our mindsets. Our mindsets are our resolves, our predetermined perspectives.

So, if we have a free will and science says we can determine what we allow into our mind, we can steward or control what we allow to influence us. We have a choice, so let's get real and use our free will wisely and let our choices be edifying to our own life and to others.

Science states there are two categories of thought; fear or love. Love will cause us to edify--- to improve or impact in moral knowledge, or to uplift, enlighten. Fear will cause us to strike out at someone or at ourselves; or to cower down, try to hide. We get to choose what will motivate us into action.

Love thoughts can be anything that is morally beneficial to ourselves or others, such as being polite, courteous, considerate, respectful, truthful and so forth. Fear thoughts can be anything stressful, such as fear of the unknown, fear of failure, inadequacy, physical inability, harm or consequence.

We are the ones who create a pattern in our lives; we create our attitudes, our mindsets. Positive thinking is a real thing; positive is uplifting and edifying. Positive thinking is love thoughts in process. Negative thinking is fear thoughts in process. We can take a couple seconds and identify a thought as fear or love; then choose to accept or reject the thought before the process goes any further. Or we can allow some other influence to make that choice for us and then we live with the ramifications of those choices.

There are ramifications for everything, starting with our thought lives where the process begins. Now is the time to embrace self-discipline and control the choices that shape and drive our lives.

Just remember, you do have a choice in every situation, under every circumstance. You can't afford to forfeit your own choice. If you do, someone else will gladly use your choice to benefit them or take advantage of you.

CHAPTER 5

Widen Your Perspective

IF WE ARE STILL WONDERING WHY WE SHOULD BE SO CONCERNED about what is influencing us and what choices we are making, think of it this way; the lives we are living are the result of the choices we have made, and the choices we have made are the result of the greatest influences in our lives.

We have already stated that the main sources of influences can be divided into three categories: our self—through the lusts and desires of our own mind and flesh; other people or the ways of the world; unseen or spiritual urging and leading.

In one of my studies I found a comparison between a *captive* and a *prisoner.* A Captive was described as a person who has been imprisoned through lies and deceptions, or someone who believes lies. A Prisoner was described as a person whom a judge has sentenced to jail for criminal activity, or someone who lives an immoral or illegal lifestyle. Simply put, we can be a captive or one imprisoned by the lies of another person or form of influence. This is also known as bondage (defined from a term for slavery) so, we can become a slave to the will of someone else or some influence, forfeiting our own control over our lives or choices.

The influences we believe and our thought lives can make us a captive! That's enough to make you stand up and take notice. There are consequences for what we allow into our minds. What we allow into our minds makes its way into our hearts, and what is in our hearts is manifested in our actions and our communication. We can be in bondage working as slaves for an agenda we are not even aware of or for something we never agreed with.

- Radicalization and mob-mentality are a direct consequence to outside influences.
- Entitlement and self-justification are a direct consequence to our own insecurities.
- Hatred and revenge are a direct consequence to an unseen or spiritual influence.
- A mistake repeated more than once is a decision.

Is it getting easier to see why we must take control of our own lives, our own thoughts?

Many people claim they do not believe in God and they do not believe in Satan. The people who say they do not believe in God, recognize that there is a Higher Power or a Supreme Being, but they don't want to be subject to or accountable to this Being so they just deny the existence. The people who say they don't believe in Satan, recognize that there is evil in the world but don't want to acknowledge that some unseen force can cause them harm.

To make a point let's just say there is a God and a Devil—there are enough references and accounts of both to substantiate existence. Checking dictionaries, encyclopedias, concordances, and other references will give you an understanding of the character and purpose or agenda of each.

These are the main two spiritual influences we have to deal with. So, let's take a look at what some of these references say about who Satan is and why he wants to influence us into a destructive life style. It's always good to know what we are dealing with.

We have talked about influences as positive and negative, good and evil, a live force or spirit, subtle or obvious, habits and motives, manipulation and blackmail, and culture or tradition. Digging deeper and looking at sources of these types of influences, we find one which we call Satan, or the devil, the evil one, the enemy, the dark spirit, whatever we want to call him.

So, before we start rejecting thoughts that come to our minds or turn off our brains, let me help you eliminate the unknown aspect of this negative force. We don't have to be a church goer to realize that there is a lot of evil in this world, or to understand that someone or something is constantly influencing people in the world to do evil or negative things.

Just take a look at some of the documented descriptions of who Satan is, then decide. We are taught in Sunday school … *For our struggles are not against flesh and blood, but against the rulers, against the authorities, against the powers of this dark world and against the spiritual forces of evil in the heavenly realms.* (Ephesians 6:12)

Your enemy does exist. Satan began as a beautiful angel of God, Lucifer, but after he said, *"I will raise my throne above the stars of God…"* (Isaiah 14:13). He was cast out of heaven down to the pit. An angel is a spiritual being, Lucifer was the most beautiful and crafty of all, yet pride caused him to desire to, *"make myself like the Highest".* (Isaiah 14:14) This caused his expulsion from heaven (being kicked out). Now a prideful sore loser, *"roaming the earth seeking whom he may devour".* (I Peter 5:8)

That is the short version of who he is and what his purpose is. Let's get a more detailed look at his character so we can get an idea of the negative outcome of his influence on people.

(I will reference bible scriptures that detail existence, character and purpose):

- He was a sinner from the beginning according to I John 3:8
- He was cast out of heaven. Luke 10:18
- He was cast down to hell. Isaiah 14:15
- As a (influencing) serpent, causes the fall of man. Genesis 3:1
- He was cursed by God. Genesis 3:14
- He tested Jesus. Matthew 4:3-10
- He desired to "have" the apostles. Luke 22:31
- He seeks whom he may devour. I Peter 5:9
- He is subtle. Genesis 3:1
- He is presumptuous. Job 1:6
- He is cruel. Luke 8:29
- He is deceitful. II Corinthians 11:14
- He is powerful. Ephesians 2:2
- He is proud. I Timothy 3:6
- He is wicked. I John 2:13
- He perverts the scripture. Matthew 4:66
- He is the father of all lies. John 8:44

So, don't deceive yourselves, our enemy is real, he is smart, he has powers, and he wants to destroy us. But the battle is not lost, nor is it what we would presume. It is a spiritual battle that must be understood and fought against as such. We can be prepared and not deceived.

The battle starts in our minds, that is his battle field. He starts by influencing us to his way of thinking, by twisting or distorting the truth, by encouraging despair. He steals our hope of the future, our joy, peace and rest. He wears us down and puts us in bondage.

His job and purpose are to provide the temptation or lies, it is our job to reject him and his tactics. Reject his thoughts of fear or anger, don't let it get in our minds and hearts. We deal with this influence the same way we deal with all the other sources of influence we have talked about. But we must be aware and we must make the right choices, it is up to us.

Satan merely talked to Eve and convinced her to listen to him not God who said, *"don't eat from that one tree"*. Satan may have been talking to her off and on for a long time, got her to trust him, he may have even taken a bite of the fruit himself and said, *"see it is good to eat, try it"*. He just needed to insert some doubt into her convictions. (Genesis 3:1-6)

His influence had become more substantial and relative at the time than anyone else's. Suddenly Eve saw in her mind that the fruit of the tree was good for food, it was pleasing to the eyes and desirable for obtaining wisdom, so she gave in to Satan's influence and convinced Adam to do the same.

Scripturally, who you yield yourself to becomes your 'lord' or authority in your life. Consequently, the dominion and authority over the world that God had given to Adam now belonged to Satan. Adam and Eve became subject to the will and ways of their new 'lord'. Satan's authority can be considered the fear thoughts that come to our mind as his influence caused catastrophic consequences to the lives of Adam and Eve as well as mankind. (Genesis 3:16-19)

On the other hand, the other spiritual influence, God, represents the love thoughts that come to our mind. This is identified by looking at the characteristics and purpose of God. The main thing said about Him, *God is Love*, I John 4:16. He is our Creator and Father. The very nature of a father is to provide for and to protect his children.

As *His children,* man was created for relationship with God. He created the *Garden of Eden* and filled it with natural beauty, four rivers, fruit and vegetables plants and trees, animals and everything else to fulfill every need of man. No toil, danger or sickness was present. Then He created man and gave him dominion over the earth. This was the love and provision of God, He created mankind (gave him life) with the purpose of having a (loving) relationship or connection and He put everything in the garden that man could need to survive and be comfortable,

But man gave away dominion over the earth to Satan by putting the words of Satan higher than the words of God (who you yield yourself to –obey—becomes your Lord). Satan unleashed his character and purpose (of destruction) upon man and the world created by God, thus the evil we experience in the world today. The spiritual influence of Satan and his evil intent is intertwined throughout the entire world we live in.

Just as Adam and Eve had a free will choice to make while in the garden, we have a choice to make in our lives, accept or reject the thoughts injected into our minds, consider the type of thought, the source and the ramifications. Don't shrug off personal accountability, because it affects your entire life and the lives of everyone you love and all of mankind.

Evil is alive and well in this world. How we allow this evil to affect our attitudes and perspective will then affect future generations through the influence we pass down to them. This is an ongoing battle not just a battle during our lifetimes. Your accountability today projects into the future.

Look at the evil progression on our own Country's governmental process (as talked about in a previous chapter). The influence of negative or evil thinking has morphed our society into one of judging and labeling people, hating and smearing others, destroying and stealing and manipulating what is true and what is a lie. It is the same negative influence progressing over a long period of time into something that is now evil.

CHAPTER 6

How to Process

LET'S DO A SELF-EXAMINATION, A REALITY CHECK OF OUR OWN behaviors, just for our own information and insight. Looking at some of the behavior's influences can bring into our lifestyle, can we see a lifestyle, habit or characteristics in ourselves that we never acknowledged or recognized before? Now, try to trace these back to; what, when, where, why, and how. Are these actions or characteristics in our lives from our own strong desires (lusts) or our own feelings of entitlement or being correct (pride)? Or can we trace them back to an outside source? Or are they from an unknown source?

Being real with yourself is the only way to regain any ability to direct your own life. Not looking at yourself or addressing behavior doesn't change anything. Maybe you are saying you don't need to change anything, that shows that you have already been influenced not to question your behavior or beliefs. And the cycle continues.

You aren't doing anything for someone else, you are doing this for yourself. You want to be the best you can be, the most successful you can be, the happiest and most content you can be. All of this depends on the correct, conscious choices you are making. Your choices determine your life. And don't forget your life affects everyone around you, especially the ones closest to you.

You can lie to others, you can hide from others, you can even lie to yourself, but you can't hide from yourself. You have to live the life you are creating. You subject the life you created onto your family and loved ones. Analyzing your own behavior is like peeling layers off of an onion, there are layers after layers of influences, beliefs and fears that make up who you are. If you want to change anything, improve anything or gain anything you have to understand what is already motivating you. Why do you feel like that, why do you think like that?

Example: Why do you feel sad? Because I feel all alone. Why do you feel all alone? Because I don't let people close to me/ don't spend time with people. Why don't you let people close to you? Because I am afraid, they won't like me. Why are you afraid they won't like you? Because I don't want to feel rejected. Why would you feel rejected? Have you ever felt rejected before? Layer after layer, it can take time to uncover the root of a conviction or perspective.

You can change the way you feel. You can change the way you think. You can change the way you react and respond. It all takes time and effort; it is all determined on your choices. You can go to a secular counselor or therapist. But a psychiatrist cannot heal you, cannot fix you, cannot change you. This is up to you.

A psychiatrist is trained to provide a safe place for you to talk, the more you talk the more you remember, you awaken the sub-conscious. What you do with your memories and feelings is up to you and it will affect your future. Another way a safe place is established is by assuring you that you can't be judged because you are a victim. Being a victim frees you from any accountability for your part or your actions. Being a victim becomes an excuse for continued harmful behavior (through entitlement). If you are a victim you have no expectation of change or accountability. This is not to say that at some point you were not a victim to some unwanted influence or activity or association. But continuing to be a victim can become an excuse. Excuses prevent us from actually dealing with situations and problems.

Many people go through horrific experiences but come out determined to be better than before (physically, mentally or emotionally). I have seen people that have lost their limbs yet they are still out there giving motivational speeches or setting new records in sporting events. It is all determined by their choice not to throw their life away but to do something positive with it. The term, *positive thinking,* is real and powerful. Your determination, what you allow to harbor in your mind motivates your choices. You have the privilege of choice.

That choice doesn't stop at your thoughts, what you initially allow into your mind, now it continues through your actions and plans and every day of your like. You must continue to purposely and consciously live your life. Being accountable for your actions and choices is not a negative thing, it is privilege and a necessity. You determine your future through your choices today. Don't give in to influences, don't emotionally react to situations, don't fold under pressure.

CHAPTER 7

Aware or Unaware

SO, YOU REALIZE THERE IS INFLUENCE ALL AROUND YOU, AND YOU have to take the time and effort to analyze and then accept or reject the thoughts that come into your mind. You need to develop a disciplined thought life by being aware of what you are allowing into your mind. You have a choice to make. One of the things that will help you to do this is your attitude.

Your attitude is a pre-determined resolve or strong decision (like: 'No matter what I will never give up'). You subconsciously create boundaries, you draw the line, you establish the stopping point for yourself before you get to a situation requiring you to take a stand.

There are good (positive) attitudes and bad (negative) attitudes. Obviously, these attitudes will drive your life into a predictable direction. Again, this is why you must consciously live every day of your life. You must be accountable to yourself. No accountability, no acknowledgment of where your life is taking you. It seems simple but just like influences, we don't always see what is directing or leading us. We can't always see ourselves. We aren't always conscious of our own life.

If you can develop some good, strong, positive attitudes you will have an upper hand in making good choices. You won't default to negative thinking or fear-based reactions so often. A positive attitude can act like a shield, deflecting harmful choices or reactions, setting you up to deal with the issues that challenge you. Challenges or resistance are opportunities to strengthen or improve yourself, all you need is the right attitude.

Strengthening or improvement in any area of your life (physical or mental) requires effort or work on your part to create the change. Change doesn't happen automatically; it requires you to do something. The right attitude empowers you (through your resolve) to address or handle what-ever issue you are facing. Stress becomes a factor when you don't address the issues in your life.

Stress is the cousin of fear, it hinders you or paralyzes you so you won't move forward. Stress is an open door to sickness and disease; it triggers your brain to release chemicals and hormones into the body that in return cause physical inability in the body. Stress is a spirit that stops you physically, mentally and spiritually in your tracks. Stress is a physical manifestation of a fear thought that entered your mind and you allowed into your brain. Stress is you not facing and correcting the issue in your life then forming the wrong attitude.

Your attitude is a mirror of your personality. Your personality is the essence of who you are, the combination of characteristics or qualities that form your distinctive character, what your life represents. Your character represents the mental and moral qualities distinctive to you as an individual. Your personality is a sign around your neck saying how you will react to a situation, a conversation, a single word of opinion, it tells on you. You can think in your own mind that you are this or that type of person but your personality has already told on you. Your attitude is a manifestation of your personality. Everything is linked together so be careful what your thoughts and choices are saying about you to others.

Stop shying away from personal accountability. How else will you know what you have allowed to slip into your mind and choices. How can you ever take back control of your own life? Accountability is not a bad word. Attitude is not always a good thing. Personality is a real and factual account of who you are and how you handle yourself and situations that come up in your life. And all of these are predetermined by the influences you have chosen to heed to. Simply put attitude is how you act (towards and around other people).

What you have allowed to influence you is now influencing others about you. You had a choice about what influences you accepted or rejected, that directly shaped you into who you are and that directly influences others perception of you. Your choices have gone full circle.

It is your responsibility to 'steward' what you allow to dictate your personality, character and actions. Stewardship is the job of taking care of something. No stewardship always results in undesired and negative consequences. So, newsflash—it's on you! How you respond to every good and bad thing that comes your way determines the quality of the life you live and what your personality/character has become. YOU ARE WHAT YOU DECIDE

Don't let someone else decide who you are. This is done most subtly through our relationships. One example is a relationship where one constantly and continually puts down or ridicules another. An ongoing harassment or destruction of someone's opinion, character or self-worth. If you are told every day "you're wrong", "you don't know", "you can't...", "you'll never...", after awhile you will start to believe it. This leaves you vulnerable to the one putting you down.

This can be called emotional abuse, emotional blackmail, grooming, forced submission or usury.

This is a direct attack on your self-worth, self-confidence and self-esteem.

If you are in a relationship where the other person constantly tells you that you are wrong, or they don't value your opinion, step back and take a long look. What are you allowing to happen to your self-worth? Are you stewarding your own life or is someone/something else?

Character abuse can happen when someone is constantly talking about someone else to you, complaining about them, purposely trying to get you to look at that person negatively. You must ask yourself why are they doing this, what is in it for them (this is called 'throwing dirt')? Are they trying to exalt themselves in your eyes? Are they trying to reveal something? Are you now influenced by that opinion?

Why are you so afraid to trust your own opinion of someone else but eagerly accept another's characterization of other people? Are you trying to be liked or accepted by them? Are you trying to fit in? Is there a promised benefit for you to just agree? So, outside influence has won again! And someone else is demonized because of that influence.

CHAPTER 8

What Now

SO, WHAT DO WE DO NOW?

Quit making excuses
Quit justifying
Quit blaming others
Quit playing the victim card

Let's Get Real – you need to get real with yourself – take back control and the deciding factors in your life. It is your life and your choice. Take over the stewardship of your life. Be accountable. Be free and undeterred. Be confident and rational. Don't be afraid to seek knowledge and clarity before making decisions and choices. Be informed.

To be the things listed above you have to be honest with yourself. You have to take on the burden of being informed and knowledgeable in regards to the choices you have to make. Don't just follow the crowd, that crowd could be a mob leading you into disaster.

You need to identify yourself to yourself. You need to like yourself. Give yourself a "self-examination". Make note of your weaknesses and of your strengths; your fears and your aspirations. You need to know who you are, what your challenges are, and where you want to go or be, before you can make necessary choices to help you get there.

Determine now what you want in the end, then start building the road (through your choices) that will take you there.

It sounds "that easy", but is it? We have looked at only a few of the influences vying for not only your choices but for your life. It is that serious! But you are the one who has the ability to do something about it, to steward your life in a way that is victorious.

There is a culture driven by subliminal messaging and social standards that alter our choices in every stage of our life that may not direct us to a path towards victorious living. It's hard to believe, and many of us don't want to believe we can be that vulnerable or naïve.

Let's consider a few more examples of the influences or cultures that lead us away from the victorious life we are looking for:

Marriage—most of us look forward to getting married one day and creating a family and a future. But society says, "you don't have to get married…"; "you don't have to put up with that…"; "just get out…". The divorce rate is well over 60%; commitment is a fading word; relationship has lost honor and respect, or even expectation. Is this a victorious life?

Debt—we want everything now and we want it weather we can afford it or not. Lending institutions bombard you with credit card offers (with interest rates tickling 30%), they even offer you tens of thousands of bonus points for some gift system IF you charge upwards to $4000.00 in the first 60-90 days of opening your new account. The average American spends 130% of their annual income. Did you plan to get into debt so badly that you have to borrow money to pay your bills? Does this look victorious?

Obesity—being overweight is a health hazard that stems (from one of many issues) from the culture of fellowshipping over food/eating, from the entitlement of pleasure food or comfort food, from processed/chemical and sodium filled food. Obesity is beyond overweight, yet 40% + of the American population is obese. I can't imagine many (or any) people trying to become obese. Does this sound like a victorious life?

We could go on but I think you can get the picture. What is considered normal isn't always victorious. Let's Get Real.

And while we are at it let's get over the notion that everything we read or hear in any form of media is truth and factual. If it is 'people' who are easily influenced who are posting and reporting on media platforms, how can we put our confidence in what is being 'fed' to us. What are you digesting?

It has even been shown that with technology they can mix whatever message they want with the voice and image of whomever they think you will trust and believe. You just need a little truth mixed with a lot of hype or sensationalizing to create a completely different and believable scenario.

You can see why so many people just go with the flow. It takes a lot of time and work to steward your life, but it is your life, isn't it? You can't afford to take anything at face value or for granted. That would be like giving the keys to your car to someone who may not have a driver license or insurance and hope nothing happens leaving you liable. You are responsible for the choices you make. Not only that, but you are responsible for how your choices impact the life of your family, your boss, your business partner, those closest to you. Your choices don't affect just you. Your choices even affect your children's adult life and your children's children.

I'm sure there are some who are saying, 'So what?', 'What does it matter?'. One word – Purpose. Does your life have a purpose?

First, consider this, science concludes that mankind was created with a 'love' nature. It is our nature to choose edifying or love actions and thoughts. So, fear thoughts must come from another influence. And if we were created with a 'love' nature, we must have a purpose to edify or uplift in a positive way.

Have you considered the purpose of your life? Do you have purpose? Do you want purpose? Want it or not there is purpose in your life. That purpose can be enhanced or destroyed by the choices you make, by the influences you concede to, or by the conscious stewardship of your thought life.

We all have a life to live, and a purpose for that life. So, if you have a life you must live, wouldn't you want to have a positive or edifying purpose? If so, choose that, work towards that, put forth the effort to achieve that. You have the ability to do this. You need to develop a positive mindset. Sometimes this requires a renewing of your mind.

How do we renew our mind? It is possible but it takes effort and time. You must be aware of your current mindset and deliberately decide to change it. You have probably heard that it takes 30 days to change a habit, well actually it takes longer than that. You must practice not doing the habit you want to break (don't react—but respond), take a few seconds to think before you react to your automatic habit. After you have done this, then you have to replace that action/habit with the response you want and deliberately practice that repetitively for it to become your renewed behavior or habit.

This is called stewarding your life. We all have a responsibility to be a good steward over our own life and the choices we make. This is what affects the quality and direction of our life and the effect or influence we project on other people's life. Our choices, our mindset, our personal perspective all shape us into who we are and how we act and react, how we interact with others. Consciously living our lives and stewarding our choices is the key to being able to have a positive and purposeful life. Otherwise you are just riding down a conveyor belt and someone else is using your life for their agenda. It is up to you.

Learning the effects of influence on your life is meant to be a wakeup call for you. It is never too late to take back your life if you find you have subconsciously lost control. The bigger question is, do you want to be responsible for your own life? Do you want your life to have purpose? Do you want to live a victorious or productive (edifying) life? Everything has a price, and so does being the leader of your own life instead of a follower of other's influence on your life.

CHAPTER 9

Stewardship

IN OUR PLAN OF ACTION, WE NEED TO LOOK CLOSER TO THE "stewardship" of our own life and the "renewing" of our own mind. To help our understanding we should start with a simple definition of the two words:

Stewardship – the act of managing or supervising of something careful and responsible management of something entrusted to one' s care

Renewing – to make new, fresh or strong again to restore, regenerate or replace

So, it seems that stewarding your life and renewing your mind requires some deliberate accountability on your part. Looking at synonyms of these two words you will find such things as; governance, guidance, overseeing, administration, restoring, and rejuvenating to name a few. All of these action words may make you feel overwhelmed or inadequate, but you were created with the ability and free will choice you need to accomplish stewardship of your own life and renewing of your own mind. We can't just go along blindly with the crowd, with today's hype, we need to use our free will choice wisely.

As read/written previously, it all starts with our thought life. We must take the time to question our every thought and how that thought will affect our physical life. Again, what we allow into our mind affects our personality, character, emotional wellbeing and even our health. Our thoughts are manifested through our actions and opinions.

You don't need to put a lot of pressure on yourself, you don't need to be afraid of failure, but you can't be complacent. Failure is just a process of elimination (well, now I know, what you don't know or don't learn from your experiences you will repeat (your failures). Remember, you can't control everything, but you can position yourself for a different or better outcome next time. Positioning is a form of stewarding; you are taking action to increase a desired outcome. So, consider any failure as a learning process and opportunity to improve your position (your ability to handle a particular situation or circumstance.

Complacency is when you accept the position you are in; you don't believe you can or you need to do any more or anything different; this is stunting your growth or ability. Complacency and procrastination are mental or emotional strongholds that stop or slow us down from any progress or victories. Then there is no renewing of our minds.

What you focus on is where your "interest" (some say "treasure") is; and there is where your "heart" is also (your "heart" is your conviction, your purpose, your passion/faith/confidence). Your focus can identify the area of need in your stewardship and renewing of the mind. The more you think about something, the more it will grow and eventually become habit. This can be a bad thing (as in lust and covet or fear thoughts) or a positive thing (as in being thoughtful and edifying or charitable thoughts).

Think about it, you do have the ability to manage your own life and control your own thinking.

This is an exciting thing to realize, and a victory for each and every one of us. Don't get nervous or skeptical, just start restoring the "charge" of your own life. Get a one year plan, and a five year or even a lifetime goal and purpose for your life, and get busy. Take back your life. Be intentional. Make plans to be the best that you can be. Be proud of who you are and what you have done that supports brotherly love. What a victory in action. But, if you give a voice to negative or fear thoughts, you will become a captive to those things. This will manifest in destructive outcomes, accomplishing nothing worthwhile.

A walking cane that can help us achieve the things we are talking about is simply – faith.

Just as "Positive Thinking" is a process to change our lives, faith can change our lives. The stewardship of our lives and renewing of our minds require a process, that process requires us to do something. Faith is more than just a statement, it is an action word, it requires our participation. If we think about it and have some faith, we will start to do something. Just as a farmer plants some seeds and has faith that something will grow, he continues to tend to the ground to help the process because of his expectation. Others go to a job every day because they have faith or believe they will receive a pay check at the end of the week. Faith motivates.

Faith will give us confidence and enthusiasm to work for something. We need to identify the purpose of our lives, what we want to accomplish or where we want to go. Then through faith we can use our expectation to give us the strength to do the work necessary to achieve our goal or 'purpose'. That goal is obtained by good stewardship of all our thoughts and agendas, what or who we allow to influence us. If the influence or thoughts are not our own or are not what will help us to our 'purpose', we need to reject that thought and renew our minds to a better way of thinking.

The belief system we are going to follow or work is our choice, so make an informed choice. Then we must stick with our decision, we can't afford to faulter, the price is too high. My father-in-law had many wise and humorous statements, one was: "If we don't stand for (or believe in) something, we will stoop for anything". You could say, stooping for anything is equivalent to giving in to whatever others want us to think/believe/act on. Standing for something is our resolve in our faith.

We can govern our own thoughts and choices, don't react to every influence, respond to the influence in an informed and decisive way that gives us the deciding factor. We do not have to be controlled by influences.

CHAPTER 10

Personal View

OUR OWN PERSPECTIVE IS ONE OF OUR BIGGEST INFLUENCES, especially in how we view ourselves. Our self esteem and confidence are shaped by how secure and supported we felt as we were growing up. Then as we graduated into being responsible for ourselves, our own actions and behavior, we had to choose to learn from our mistakes and take inventory of our own behavior. We can not justify negative behavior by what others did or said, but we must take accountability for our own actions. Facing our fears, dealing with our situations and circumstances might be hard but it reinforces our confidence and self-esteem.

Shrugging things off and pointing fingers actually robs us of self-worth. When we can feel good about ourselves and respect ourselves, we become more confident and create faith in our lives.

Faith is a motivator and empowerment that we can lean on when we are struggling. We can say this strong belief is explained as, 'being sure of what we hope for and certain of what we have not yet seen, so we are taking actions to move toward what we are anticipating.

We must try to become mature and start thinking about more than just our basic needs. We shouldn't spend time thinking about why we need to turn from deeds that bring negative outcomes. Let's grow-up and engage in helpful actions. If we have faith, we should be doing something that supports that faith.

A field is useful to a farmer because when seed is planted mixed with some rain, it will produce good crops. But land that only produces weeds and thorns is worthless. You could say faith is choked out by pride (replacing faith), leaving nothing to build on.

Those ruled by their desires think only of themselves. When we think only of ourselves it is easier to do evil or harmful things. Selfish desires will stop you from doing anything good or edifying. Let's stop for a moment and make this statement easier to recognize: How many times have the "rights" or "desires" of someone else infringed on your rights or desires?

Example: you are a non-smoker, yet a smoker believes they have a right to smoke anywhere they want because they aren't harming you (just themselves); you have to smell their smoke, breathe their second hand smoke, get the smell of smoke in your clothes/hair/furniture/curtains and even in the walls – where you work, live, go for entertainment and socializing. You can not give special rights to one group without infringing on the rights of another group.

If our belief-system is a working process it takes steps and time (deeds or actions and patience). Sometimes undesired circumstances or resistance comes up or gets in our way, but we can't just give-up or give-in. Life goes on. Challenges build endurance, endurance builds character which builds hope (or our faith).

If this system or process has something tangible supporting it like testimonies or evidence of positive outcome our faith and confidence will continue to increase. All of this gives us power to steward our own life and outcome. This confidence or power must be stewarded in a good or positive direction so all our effort and actions do not produce weeds and thorns and therefor become useless.

If our life has purpose, an intended plan or aim, shouldn't we be influenced by that? What our faith is in should agree with what is influencing us. Take a moment right now and identify or review our purpose. Now list the things that are influencing our lives, mark the influences that agree with our purpose and 'X' those influences that resist or disagree with our purpose.

We know our faith system can help us protect and achieve our purpose. Yet many of us fight against attaching that belief in or to God. To some of us God is that outside influence that we do not want to give-in to because we think we have to give up something, or we do not want to be accountable for our own choices and life style. Avoiding or ignoring something doesn't make it go away. We might be missing out on the very thing we need to achieve all we really want.

There really is not a true agnostic or atheist, these are just self-righteous individuals justifying their own refusal of personal accountability. There are too many recorded facts and accounts that support the existence of a higher power; too many unexplainable occurrences that are credited to a miracle (spiritual intervention). Even a large portion of the Scientific community now agrees there is a higher level of spiritual power (God) that exists and is connected to the creation of the world as we know it and mankind.

Believing in God will not cause us to lose anything, we will still have free choice and self-will.

Not believing in God is causing us to forfeit benefits and assistance in all of our challenges. So why wouldn't we afford ourselves the option to revisit the possibility of His existence?

God and recorded history supporting His existence where here long before the labels or definition of an atheist or an agnostic. (Who came first, the chicken or the egg?) God did!

We think we know God but we don't, we merely know of God but we have no idea who He is. The only thing we know is someone else's' perspective of God; someone else's' rejection of Him because of their own hardships or disappointments.

Let's not cut ourselves short because of someone else's negativity or pain. Let's find out for ourselves who this God really is, then make an informed choice to accept or reject this 'truth'. God is a gentleman; He won't force Himself on anyone. On the other hand, Satan constantly disguises himself to infiltrate our minds and poison our perspective of God and steal our faith and freedom. (Go back and read the second half of chapter 5)

We don't have to admit to anyone if we take the time to re-examine our understanding and conclusion or belief in this arena. It is our choice; or have we surrendered our will to the will of another already? Is it too late? No, it is never too late. What's holding us back? What are we afraid of?

We need to know that in ancient world history there are multiple accounts of the man, Jesus, and the miraculous things he did during his lifetime. There are even accounts of his appearance and engagement with others after his crucifixion on the cross. His life impacted the world so much that the calendar was dated according to his life; time before his life is recorded as BC – Before Christ; time after his public life is recorded as AD – After Death (of Christ on the cross). This calendar of time is still being used today throughout the entire world.

This one true God is the only living god; all other entities referred to as a god either were never a living person or have died and have never been heard from since. This God is identified as our Creator and Father. If we have a problem in our lives wouldn't we want the creator to help fix it, He would know better than anyone; or wouldn't we want to consult our father if we were confused about something. A creator and a father have an invested interest in our success. Who better to influence our lives, help us understand ourselves, give us insight on stewarding our lives? Faith in this invested partner could increase our success and victories.

Give Him the benefit of a doubt. Let's give ourselves the opportunity to know Him, not just know of Him. Find out who He really is and what His connection is with us. The only way to do this is to take the time to build a relationship with Him, like any other relationship this takes deliberate time and effort on our part. Relationships don't happen, they are created through investing ourselves into others.

If our car broke down wouldn't we want to take it to a Dealership or Mechanic certified by the manufacturer or creator of that car to get the best possible assistance in correcting the problem? Don't our 'Life' issues deserve the same expertise?

We have a choice today! Will we consciously steward our life or go with the crowd? Will we walk in discipline and dignity or in lust and self-entitlement? We really can't afford to be guilty of wrongful acts, bitterness or unforgiveness. We can't be careless with our own life; it affects more than just us.

We have a choice today! One day that choice will affect our ability to govern our own life and our relationships with our fellow-man/woman. That choice could assist us in transforming oppression and bondage into freedom and justice.

We have a choice today! That choice could result in our influence over our own family and children to be confident with-in themselves and considerate of others. We should encourage building character as well as celebrating good character in others.

We have a choice today! Will that choice take us down a crooked path or a straight-way to success and prosperity? Will we obtain peace, joy and rest; or will we lose our hope and faith? Will we be able to transform the world around us, create true brotherhood and be free at last.

COMING SOON!

Bio

LINDA RAINWATER IS A PASTOR, MINISTRY Co-Founder, Ministry Administrator with over 35 years' experience in various non-profit organizations. Described as a scribe, historian and an "office firefighter", she has set up and created policies and procedures for manufacturing and service companies, as well as written curriculum for non-profit education. She believes policies set today should benefit procedures later. As a speaker she has a passion to encourage others to be all they were purposed to be by using their choices and actions in positive, progressive ways. Your choice is a tool in determining your future.

Linda and her husband Jesse have been married 55 years and have raised their four children together; enjoy 12 grandchildren and five great-grandchildren.

CPSIA information can be obtained
at www.ICGtesting.com
Printed in the USA
FSHW020047250121
77840FS

9 781662 805073